OZAIN

The Secrets of Congo Initiations& Magic Spells

PALO MAYOMBE - PALO MONTE - KIMBISA

AMERICAN CANDOMBLE CHURCH PUBLICATIONS, LOS ANGELES

OZAIN

The Secrets of Congo Initiations & Magic Spells

PALO MAYOMBE - PALO MONTE - KIMBISA

AMERICAN CANDOMBLE CHURCH
P.O. BOX 881377
LOS ANGELES, CALIFORNIA 90009

TABLE OF CONTENTS

THE SPIRIT OZAIN

INTRODUCTION

The origins and the sacred mysteries of the spirit Ozain are believed to have come to Earth on a meteorite.The spirit Ozain is pictured as a grossly disfigured individual having one arm and sometimes only one leg. The spirit Ozain is also known to have a tiny ear and one extremely large ear. The spirit Ozain can only hear through his small ear in which the birds communicate directly with him. The birds are the sacred messengers of the spirit Ozain. The spirit Ozain did not always look like this and there are several stories and histories of how this came about. The spirit Ozain is regarded by the initiates of the Congo religions of Palo Mayombe, Palo Monte and Kimbisa as a powerful wizard who knows all of the magical secrets that each and every herb and plant contains.

The spirit Ozain is syncretized by initiates of the Congo religious traditions with the Catholic Saints; *San Ramon Donato*, *San Silvestre* and *St. Joseph*.

Although this book only contains the sacred ritual formula of how to prepare the "***Fundamento of Ozain***", there are various spiritual paths of the spirit Ozain. All of the spiritual paths of the spirit Ozain are associated with herbs, healing and the secrets of how to perform powerful magical spells and rituals. The following are some of the spiritual paths worshiped and venerated by the initiates of the Congo religious tradition;

Ozain Agé - This particular spiritual path of the spirit Ozain is known as the great sorcerer, knowing all the medicines, mainly of the secrets that hide in the pumpkin or squash. This particular spiritual path of the spirit Ozain lives at the foot of tall leafy trees and within the vines.

Ozain Bi - This particular spiritual path of the spirit Ozain has dealings with the Aje Spirit, *Iyami Osorongá* and the birds. This particular spiritual path of the spirit Ozain is a great magician and herbalist.

Ozain Ajube - This particular spiritual path of the spirit Ozain is known as a great healer. This particular spiritual path of the spirit

Ozain heals ailments related to internal organs (liver, intestines, stomach, etc).

Ozain Beremi - This particular spiritual path of the spirit Ozain works on the banks of rivers with abundant vegetation.

Ozain Oloógun - This particular spiritual path of the spirit Ozain is an excellent herblist and the owner of all the medicines.

According to historical texts used by the initiates of the Congo religious tradition, the spirit Ozain was disfigured in a war that he had with the Yoruba diety, Shango. According to African myths, the diety, Shango went to the diety, Orula (the Yoruba diety of divination)to spiritually consult the Sacred Oracle of Ifa to find out why he was having such bad luck. Upon doing the divination, Orula determined that someone was doing powerful witchcraft to Shango. Although Orula knew that the spirit Ozain was doing the witchcraft to Shango, he did not tell Shango who was doing it. Orula only told Shango about how to do a powerful spiritual remedy (Ebo) to remove the witchcraft from around him.

Orula knew that the spirit Ozain had done the witchcraft to Shango because Ozain knew that Shango wanted to steal the magical secrets of the herbs from him. Orula told Shango that if he wanted to remove the witchcraft that he would have to prepare a magical oil lamp which he could use for protection. Orula instructed Shango how to prepare the magical oil lamp. Orula told Shango that the lamp had to be made using twelve lightning stones, cotton wicks and almond oil. Orula explained to Shango that by preparing and burning the magic oil lamp that it would destroy the black magic being sent his way and chase down the person who was responsible for doing it.

Shango went to the highest mountain peak and prepared the magical oil lamp. As he lighted the last cotton wick, the magic lamp caused a great thunder storm to take place. The spirit Ozain took cover from the strong thunder storm under the roof of a wooden shack. The lightning began to strike down many trees around the wooden shack that the spirit Ozain was hiding in. The thunder storm got worse until finally lightning struck the side of the mountain and the rocks tumbled down on top of the spirit Ozain crushing him. This is one myth of how the spirit Ozain became permanently disfigured. This is also why all sons of the deity, Shango must receive the mysteries of the spirit Ozain.

The initiation ritual into the mysteries of the spirit Ozain is one of the most important religious ceremonies that can be received by a Palero Priest. The spiritual force of the spirit Ozain is both feared and revered by religious initiates of the Congo religious traditions of Palo Mayombe, Palo Monte and Kimbisa. The spirit Ozain is an African deity whose power lays in the use of nature, specifically in the plant world, in regards to plants and trees. The spirit Ozain lives among the trees and plants of the mountains, forest and the jungles. The spirit Ozain is the rightful owner of all vegetation found here on Earth. The sacred tree of the spirit Ozain is the CeibaTree.

The initiation ritual into the mysteries of the spirit Ozain can only be received by men and or women who are no longer menstruating. This initiation ceremony gives the initiate the spiritual right to be able to work and invoke the powerful magical mysteries of the spirit Ozain.

The initiation of the spirit Ozain is very important to receive because if a Palero Priest did not have the permission to retrieve the herbs or palos needed for a spell or ritual, it would be almost certain that the magic would not work.

The spirit Ozain is invoked and used to protect individuals against bad energy, the evil eye and disease. After the individual undergoes this very important initiation ceremony where they will receive the actual "spirit mysteries" of the Congo Spirit Ozain they are then referred to as and called by the prestigious religious title “Ozainista”. An Ozainista Priest is an invaluable member of the Congo religious community.

The mysteries of the spirit Ozain are received in an extremely elaborate and lengthy ceremony which is performed at night during a full moon or new moon.

The individual who will be receiving the initiation ceremony of the "*Fundamento of Ozain*" will receive the following four sacred items during the initiation. All four sacred items are needed to magically manifest the power of the spirit Ozain.

The first is a sealed clay bowl which contains the actual spirit mysteries of Ozain. This clay dish is called ***Okobelefo***.

The second item is a hanging gourd which contains inside, the magical secrets of Ozain. This gourd is called ***Titillero***. The *Titillero*is are beautifully decorated with multicolored beads on the outside.The *Titillero* is decorated with multicolored beads because it is believed by initiates of the Congo religious traditions that the spirit Ozain was born with millions of multicolored shiny beads surrounding his body.

The third item is a wooden doll of the spirit Ozain which also contains the mysteries sealed inside. This doll is called ***Aroni***. The *Aroni* resembles the spirit Ozain after he became disfigured.

The fourth item is called ***Orere*** (Ozun de Ozain). The *Orere* is a metal wrought iron staff about 12 inches in height which is surmounted by the wrought iron heads or complete wrought iron bodies of birds. The *Orere* is the magical staff of the spirit Ozain that predicts when danger is near. The birds are believed to be the sacred messengers of the spirit Ozain. The ***Titillero*** is hung directly over the ***Okobelefo***. The **Aroni** stands directly behind or in front of the ***Okobelefo***. The ***Orere*** is placed next to the ***Okobelefo***.

The process of making a "*Fundamento of Ozain*" is a lengthy process and takes many days to completely gather all of the necessary sacred items to correctly construct an Ozain. Ozain is believed to the "*Father of all Paleros*" and therefore the spirit Ozain is constructed in a similar method of making an nganga for the Congo nkisi spirits. The spirit Ozain is made from various herbs, palos, animals, dirts from different locations and human bones. All of these items must be gathered on the proper days and times by an experienced initiated Ozainista Priest to obtain the maximum magical power.

Before the ritual begins, a large feast is held in honor of the spirit Ozain to prepare the individuals for the ceremony. After the feast, the individuals will be instructed on what they can and can't do during the religious ritual. The initiates will then be blindfolded and led into a forest where the initiation will take place because that's where the spirit Ozain lives. The initiates are then asked to kneel down in a large hole. The hole is usually about waist deep. In each of their hands, the "*Fundamento of Ozain*" will be placed. The other items are also placed around them, along with many candles. The Ozainista Priest begins the initiation ceremony by reciting the long prayers of the spirit Ozain along with singing the ritual songs or mambos. When the spirit of Ozain hears this, he is usually fast to respond by sending a very strong wind and starts to shake the trees all around the ritual area. After the ritual prayers and songs are finished, the following animals are sacrificed and fed to each of the initiate's new "*Fundamento of Ozain*"; quails, guinea hens, roosters and a turtle. The blood from each of these animals is placed into the mouths of the initiates to taste. One water turtle is also place alive inside of the ***Okobelefo***. After the animals have been ritually sacrificed, the initiates will then place the ***Okobelefo*** of the spirit Ozain directly in front of them in the hole. Each of the initiates will then give themselves a rompemiento cleansing by tearing off their clothes and then leaves them in the holes. The tearing of their clothes signifies the act of spiritual rebirth, spiritual transformation and spiritual cleansing. The initiates will then be ritually washed in an omiero herb bath sacred to the spirit Ozain. After bathing with the sacred omiero herbal bath, the initiates will get out of the hole and then bury the complete "*Fundamento of Ozain*" along with their clothes. A white candle is placed on the dirt mound. The "*Fundamento of Ozain*" is left there for nine days and nine nights. After the nine days and nine nights, the complete "*Fundamento of Ozain*" is unearthed, cleaned and then fed again.

By completing this sacred initiation process, the spirit Ozain will be ready to use to perform powerful magical spells and rituals. When an individual receives the initiation of the spirit Ozain, it gives them a strong protection against witchcraft. The spirit Ozain also gives the new initiates the spiritual right to prepare powerful magical herbal medicines and herbal healing baths baths. When an individual receives the "*Fundamento of Ozain*", they also receive a magical symbol or sigil which can be used to invoke the powerful mysteries of the spirit Ozain. This magical symbol is called "*firma*" in the Spanish language which means signature. This sacred sigil is the magical key to bring the divine power of the spirit Ozain down to Earth. Although all of the "*Fundamento of Ozain*"are prepared in the same manner, the magical spirit sigil will differ according to the path of Ozain which walks with the new initiate. These magical spirit sigils are usually drawn on the ground in front of the "*Fundamento of Ozain*" when the Ozainista Priest wants to summon the spirit for any spiritual request.

THE RELIGIOUS FESTIVAL OF THE SPIRIT OZAIN

The day that Ozainista Priests like to perform their magical rituals on is Friday. The official religious feast day of the spirit Ozain is held on the holy religious day of *Good Friday* of each year. *Good Friday* is the only day of the year that black magic can be performed without receiving any negative consequences because it is believed that on that specific day, Jesus Christ died, descended into hell for three days and left the world unprotected. The religious festival held on *Good Friday* is one of the major feasts held within a traditional Congo Temple. The religious festival begins at 12 midnight outside at the shrine of the spirit Ozain. Only the individuals who have been initiated into the sacred mysteries of the spirit Ozain may attend to witness the ceremony. The initiates gather in front of the "*Fundamento of Ozain*"and say the invocations and sing the sacred songs to summon this powerful spirit. After the ritual is complete, the Ozainista Priest will then cleanse each of the individuals with a water turtle, guinea hen and a black rooster. These animals are then ritually sacrificed and the blood fed to all of the sacred items represented in the "*Fundamento of Ozain*". The initiates will then go to the nearest river and take a cleansing bath in the cool waters. This religious ceremony will remove any form of black magic.

.

HOW TO DO THE RELIGIOUS FESTIVAL OF OZAIN

On the religious day of *Good Friday*, an Ozainista Priest will perform a series of sacred rituals to the Congo spirit Ozain to harness and secure his power in the supernatural world.

The ceremony begins at 12 midnight and takes place at the mountains and concludes at the river with a ritual bath.

ITEMS NECESSARY

1. *THE "FUNDAMENTO OF OZAIN"*
2. *PEMBA (White Chalk)*
3. *FULA (Gun Powder)*
4. *CHAMBA*
5. *CANDLES*
6. *CIGARS*
7. *RUM*

LIVE ANIMALS NEEDED

1. *TWO BLACK ROOSTERS*
2. *TWO WATER TURTLES*

RITUAL PROCEDURE

1. The spirit signature of the Spirit of Ozain is drawn on the ground at the base of a large tree.

2. The "Fundamental of Ozain", including the wooden statue of the Congo Spirit Ozian are placed into the center of the spirit signature. The *Titillero*should be hanging from a tree branch of the large tree directly over the "Fundamental of Ozain".

3. Light the candles.

4. Recite the prayers and invocations of Ozain.

5. Ritually feed the *"Fundamento of Ozain"* the blood from all of the animals.

6. Get into the river water and bathe using African Black Soap.

7. After taking the bath in the river, change into clean white clothes.

THE INITIATION OF THE CONGO SPIRIT OZAIN

The Congo spirit Ozain is the keeper of the mysteries of the powers of the sacred magical herbs. The mysteries of the Congo spirit Ozain are received in an initiation ceremony which takes place at night. This ceremony should be performed on a full or a "New Moon" on a "Friday" evening at "12 Midnight". The ceremony takes place in heavily wooded or mountainous area and at the river.

The following ritual initiation formulas explain in full-detail how to prepare and correctly present the "*Fundamento of Ozain*". It is considered one of the major initiations of the African Congo religious tradition. There are various ceremonies and methods of in the Congo religious tradition of how to present an individual these powerful mysteries.

The following ritual ceremony of how to present the "*Fundamento of Ozain*" is how the *Montenegro Family* from Brazil has done this powerful initiation ritual of the Congo spirit Ozain for initiates in our Congo Munanzo for over 149 years with great success.

In the Montenegro Family Congo Munanzo, this initiation ceremony is done traditionally on "*Good Friday*". If your ceremony is not done similar to the following ritual initiation formula process, more than likely it wasn't done correct.

Although there are many other ritual ingredients that can be used to prepare a traditional "*Fundamento de Ozain*", the following items are the most popular. If your "*Fundamento of Ozain*" was presented to you and does not contain at least 90 % of the following sacred items, your Ozain was not made correctly.

ITEMS NECESSARY

ALL OF THE FOLLOWING SACRED INGREDIENTS MUST BE DRIED AND MADE INTO A FINE POWDER.

1. *One wooden doll of Ozain* (**ARONI**)

2. *One clay bowl with lid. The lid should have a hole about two inches in diameter size in the center* (***OKOBELEFO)***

3. *One hollow gourd (guiro)* (***TITILLERO)***

4. *One large Meteorite Stone*

5. *Nine lightning stones*

6. *Twenty-one coins from around the world*

7. *Dirt from 21 Crossroads*

8. *Dirt from the top of a Mountain*

9. *Dirt from the base of a Mountain*

10. *Dirt from the Railroad Tracks*

11. *Dirt from 12 Midnight*

12. *Dirt from 12 Noon*

13. *Dirt from the River*

14. *Dirt from the Ocean*

15. *Dirt from 21 Tombs*

16. *Dirt from a Bank*

17. *Dirt from a Forest*

18. *Dirt from a Police Station*

19. *Dirt from a Jail*

20. *Dirt from a Court*

21. *Dirt from a Hospital*

22. *Dirt from a Park*

23. *Dirt from the base of a Ceiba Tree*

24. *A piece of Gold*

25. *A piece of Silver*

26. *A piece of Copper*

27. *A piece of Bronze*

28. *7 Quartz Crystals*

29. *Powdered Bats*

30. *Powdered Snakes*

31. *Powdered Spiders*

32. *Powdered Bones & Skulls from 21 Birds of Prey*

33. *Powdered Bones & Skull from a Black Dog*

34. *Powdered Bones & Skull from a Black Cat*

35. *Powdered Chameleon Lizard*

36. *Powdered Human Skull (male)*

37. *Powdered Human Bones from various parts*

38. *Powdered Volcanic Stone*

39. *Powdered Water Turtle Bones*

40. *Dried Water Turtle Shell (whole)*

41. *The dried Head, Feet from a Water Turtle*

42. *The dried Head, Feet and Bones from a Vulture*

43. *The dried Eyes from an Owl*

44. *The dried Eyes from an Eagle*

45. *The dried Eyes from a Cat*

46. *The dried Eyes from a Dog*

47. *Twenty-One powdered Palos*

48. *121 powdered Herbs sacred to Ozain*

49. *21 seeds of "Mate Rojo"*

50. *121 seeds of "Peonia"*

51. *3 seeds of "Ojo De Buey"*

52. *Ache De Santo*

53. *The dried Heart & Head of a Rooster*

54. *The dried Heart & Head of a Hen*

55. *The dried Head & Heart of a Dove*

56. *The dried Head & Heart of a Pigeon*

57. *Powdered Egg Shell from a Chicken*

58. *Powdered Egg Shell from a Guinea Hen*

59. *The dried Head & Heart of a Guinea Hen*

60. *One pound of African Ifa Irosun Powder*

61. *The dried insides & seeds from a Squash*

62. *Dirt from a Termite Hill*

63. *Dirt from an Ant Termite Hill*

64. *Dried Scorpions*

65. *Dried Snakes*

66. *A rattle from a Rattlesnake*

67. *Dried Roots from a Vencedor Tree*

68. *Dried Roots from a Ceiba Tree*

69. *Dried Roots from a Palm Tree*

70. *Dried Roots from a Flamboyan Tree*

71. *Dried Fighting Cock Spurs*

72. *Dried Frogs*

73. *Iron Oxidate Powder & Magnetic Load Stones*

74. *Nine Red Feathers from an African Grey Parrot*

75. *Ozun De Ozain (**ORERE**)*

LIVE ANIMALS NEEDED

Nine Black Roosters
Two Guinea Hens
Two Water Turtles

PREPARING THE FUNDAMENTAL ELEMENTS OF OZAIN

PART I - PREPARING THE CLAY DISH (OKOBELEFO)

1. In a large bowl, prepare an omiero using the 121 fresh herbs of the Congo Spirit Ozain. After you have prepared the 121 herb omiero, place the Meteorite Stone along with the lightning stones to soak for a 24 hour period.

2. Light a White candle and leave it next to the items soaking in the omiero.

3. Using white paint, paint the symbol of the "*Fundamento of Ozain*" on the inside bottom of the clay bowl and then seal using candle wax.

4. After the paint has dried, wash the inside and the outside of the clay dish using the omiero.

5. Take a mouthful of rum and spray it directly into the bowl.

6. Light a cigar and blow the smoke directly into the clay bowl.

7. In a large bucket, mix all of the magical ingredients together.

8. After you have mixed all of the ingredients in the bucket, pour some of the omiero mixture with the ingredients and make a thick paste like mixture.

9. Pour all of the cement like mixture into the clay dish.

10. Place the Meteorite Stone into the center of the clay bowl and place it into the center of the cement mixture.

11. Place the nine lightning stones around the Meteorite Stone. Position the lightning stones with the larger ends are pointing outwards.

A PICTURE OF A BEADED OKOBELEFO (CLAY DISH) OF OZAIN.

PREPARING THE TURTLE SHELL

1. Using the dirt cement like mixture, stuff the turtle shell completely by packing the dirt firmly into the turtle shell.

2. Set the Turtle Shell next to the Meteorite Stone.

PREPARING THE ARONI (*MUNECO*)

(THE WOODEN OZAIN DOLL IS CALLED "ARONI")

1. Pack all of the holes on the Ozain wooden figure using the dirt cement mixture. The holes will usually be already drilled and the doll is available from any well stocked Botanica. The holes are usually in the following areas, the top of the head, under one of his arms and under one of his legs. One of the wooden dolls legs is not complete because Ozain only has one leg.

2. Place three of the feathers into the head of the doll before sealing each area with wax.

PREPARING THE OZUN DE OZAIN (ORERE)

1. The Ozun of Ozain can be placed next to the "*Fundamento of Ozain*". It should be washed in omiero and then fed a little blood from each of the sacrificed animals.

PREPARING THE GOURD (GUIRO,TITILLERO)

1. Blow cigar smoke and rum into the empty gourd to consecrate it.

2. After this, add a medium amount of the dirt cement paste mixture into the gourd.

3. Place a large lightning stone into the center of the gourd.

4. Place all of the following ingredients into the gourd; a Rattlesnake Rattle, the powdered eyes from a Black Cat, an Eagle and an Owl.

5. Place the powdered head, feet and the bones from the vulture into the gourd.

6. Place the rest of the dirt mixture into the gourd and firmly pack it in.

PREPARATION FOR THE INITIATION

ROMPEMIENTO IN THE MOUNTAINS - DAY I

1. Take the individual who will be receiving the "*Fundamento of Ozain*" to the Mountains at 12 Midnight.

2. Draw the "Fundamento symbol" of Ozain using cascarilla powder on the ground. The symbol should be large enough so that the individual can stand on top of it. Blindfold the individual.

3. Dig a large hole directly in front of the individual about 2 feet deep.

4. Light a cigar and blow the smoke over the body of the individual and inside the hole. (3 times)

5. Take a mouthful of rum and blow it over the body of the individual and inside the hole. (3 times)

6. The individual will then cleanse themselves with a mixture of 21 different types of grains. As the individual cleanses themselves they will throw the grains into the hole in front of them.

7. Take a black rooster and spiritually cleanse the individual from head to toe.

8. Pray to the Congo Spirits by speaking to the hole. After you have finished praying, sacrifice the rooster and feed the blood around the ground area which the individual is standing and also over the items in the hole.

9. Place the body of the rooster into the hole and pour honey over all of the items in the hole.

10. Begin the rompemiento cleansing ritual by tearing completely off the individual and then place all of these clothes into the hole.

11. Light a cigar and blow the smoke over the body of the individual and inside the hole. (3 times)

12. Take a mouthful of rum and blow it over the body of the individual and inside the hole. (3 times)

13. The individual will then take a bath using an omiero mixture.

14. Pour the remaining omiero mixture into the hole.

15. Cover the hole up with dirt forming a mound over all of the items in the hole.

16. Light a white candle into the center of the dirt mound.

17. Assist the individual in placing their new white clothes on.

PART 1 - ROMPEMIENTO AT THE RIVER DAY 2

1. Take the individual who will be receiving the "F*undamento of Ozain"* to the River at 12 Midnight.

2. Draw the following "Fundamento symbol"of Ozain using cascarilla powder on the ground. The symbol should be large enough so that the individual can stand on top of it. Blindfold the individual.

3. Light a white candle and present it to the following areas of the individual; top of head, their feet, their left shoulder, there right shoulder, the top of the head once again, the ground at the back of the feet, the left shoulder, the right shoulder.

4. Afterwards, give the candle to the individual in their hands and ask them to pray silently to Nzambi, to their ancestors and to the Congo spirits for blessings.

5. Light a cigar and blow the smoke over the body of the individual. (3 times)

6. Take a mouthful of rum and blow it over the body of the individual. (3 times)

7. After the individual has finished praying, take the white candle and stick it into the ground near the side of the river in the damp soil.

8. Take a black hen and spiritually cleanse the individual from head to toe.

9. Give the black hen to the individual and tell them to hold it up to their forehead and pray to their ancestors and to the Congo Spirit Ozain to seek their blessings.

10. After they have finished praying, sacrifice the hen and feed the blood around the area which the individual is standing and into the river water.

11. Place the body of the rooster near the candle and pour bee's honey over it and into the river.

12. Begin the Rompemiento by tearing the individual's clothes off and then throw the torn clothes into the river to be sweep away.

13. Light a cigar and blow the smoke over the body of the individual. (3 times)

14. Take a mouthful of rum and blow it over the body of the individual. (3 times)

15. Lead the individual by the hand into the river to bathe using African Black Soap and a handful of fresh herbs to scrub their bodies.

16. When the individual has finished, assist the individual to place on new white clothes.

PART 1 - ROMPEMIENTO AT THE CEMETERY DAY 3

1. Take the individual who will be receiving the "*Fundamento of Ozain"* to the Cemetery at 12 Midnight.

2. Draw the following "Fundamento symbol" of Ozain using cascarilla powder on the ground. The symbol should be large enough so that the individual can stand on top of it. Blindfold the individual.

3. Light a white candle and present it to the following areas of the individual; top of head, their feet, their left shoulder, there right shoulder, the top of the head once again, the ground at the back of the feet, the left shoulder, the right shoulder.

4. Afterwards, give the candle to the individual in their hands and ask them to pray silently to Nzambi, to their ancestors and to the Congo spirits for blessings.

5. Light a cigar and blow the smoke over the body of the individual. (3 times)

6. Take a mouthful of rum and blow it over the body of the individual. (3 times)

7. After the individual has finished praying, take the white candle and stick it into the ground near the tomb that has a headstone in the form of a cross.

8. Take a black hen & a black rooster and spiritually cleanse the individ-ual from head to toe.

9. Give the black hen & the black rooster one at a time to the individual and tell them to hold it up to their forehead and pray to their ancestors and to the Congo Spirit Ozain to seek their blessings.

10. After they have finished praying, sacrifice the hen, the rooster and feed the blood around the area which the individual is standing and onto the grave stone.

11. Place the body of the hen & the rooster near the candle and pour bee's honey over it and into the river.

12. Begin the Rompemiento Cleansing Ceremony by tearing the individual's clothes off and set the bodies next to the candle.

13. Light a cigar and blow the smoke over the body of the individual. (3 times)

14. Take a mouthful of rum and blow it over the body of the individual. (3 times)

15. The individual will then bathe using omiero and will scrub their bodies using 9 fresh herbs.

16. When the individual has finished, assist the individual to place on new white clothes.

THE INITIATION OF OZAIN

1. The individual who will be receiving the initiation of Ozain will be blind folded and led to the ceremonial area that will be lit up with candles.

2. A very large wide hole will be dug beforehand and the individual will be placed into the hole, standing up in the center of the hole.

3. The Congo priest presiding over the initiation ceremony will then begin the initiation ritual by first reciting the Congo prayers to the spirits and then lastly to the Congo Spirit Ozain to grant safe passage to all the members present who are attending the initiation ritual ceremony.

4. The Congo priest will then start to invoke the spirit of Ozain by singing various mambos sacred to the Congo spirit Ozain.

5. The individual will then be asked to kneel down in the center of the large hole.

6. As the individual is kneeling down, place the prepared clay dish containing the fundamental of Ozain into the individual's hands. The individual will hold the "Fundamento of Ozain" clay bowl with both hands stretched out. The Congo priest will then place a live turtle into the clay bowl and place the top on it to completely cover the fundamental of Ozain.

7. The Congo priest will then continue singing mambos to the Congo Spirit Ozain to call the powerful entity from the spirit world.

8. After the Congo priest is finished singing the songs, the individual will be asked a series of questions and to make an oath to the spirits and to his Congo Munanzo to secrecy and to honor the Tata and to uphold the honor of the Congo Spirits even if it means sacrificing their own life.

9. The Congo priest will light a cigar and blow the smoke over the body of the individual and into the hole of the clay bowl containing the fundamental of Ozain. (3 times)

10. The Congo priest will then take a mouthful of rum and blow the rum over the body of the individual and into the hole of the clay bowl containing the fundamental of Ozain. (3 times)

11. The Congo priest will then cleanse the body of individual with each of the live animals.

12. The animals are then sacrificed and the blood poured directly into the fundamental of Ozain through the hole.

13. The *Aroni,* the *Titillero* and the *Ozun De Ozain* will also be fed at the same time with the blood of the animals. These items are sitting next to the individual in the hole.

14. As each of the heads of the animals is cut off, the Congo priest will place the bloody neck of the animal into the mouth of the individual and the individual will bite down on each neck.

15. The Congo priest then carefully lifts up the lid of the clay bowl and inserts the heads of all of the animals.

16. The dead animals will be laid down next to the individual in the hole.

17. After this, the individual will be told to place the clay bowl directly in front of them.

18. The Congo priest will then do a Rompemiento cleansing on the individual and place their torn clothes in the hole next to them.

19. The Congo priest then will begin pouring omiero over the individual while singing mambos to Ozain.

20. The individual will wash their bodies using the black soap. After the ritual washing, the individual will be lifted out of the hole.

21. The items in the hole will then be covered up with dirt.

22. The Ozainista Priest will then place a white candle into the center of the dirt mound.

23. The Ozainista Priest will then blow chamba and rum directly over the entire body of the new initiate and once again blow cigar smoke over the body and other areas that the individual will receive the Ozain Initiation "cuts". Using a new razor blade, the Ozainista Priest will then cut some of the new initiate's hair and wrap it in corn hush and wrap it using thread. This special package will be placed inside of the nganga of the Spirit of Ozain that the new initiate is making the pact with in exchange for the spirits protection. The belief and theory behind doing this is that if the spirit has something of you then they will know who you are by your unique smell. It is through smell that the spirits are able to locate us because spirits can't see as we do and can only see shadows like a blind man.

The Ozainista Priest Tata then says to the initiate the following:

(Say the name of the new initiate), *You have come here today seeking the protection of the spirits.*

(Say the name of the new initiate), *May you always have a roof over your head.*

(Say the name of the new initiate), *May you always have food on your table. Sala Malekun, Malekun Sala.*

(Say the name of the new initiate), *May you always have money in your pockets. Sala Malekun, Malekun Sala.*

(Say the name of the new initiate), *May you always have good health.*

(Say the name of the new initiate), *May you always have material possessions and wealth. Sala Malekun, Malekun Sala.*

(Say the name of the new initiate), *May you never be accused by your enemies. Sala Malekun, Malekun Sala.*

(Say the name of the new initiate), *May you never be arrested. Sala Malekun, Malekun Sala.*

(Say the name of the new initiate), *May you never be placed behind bars in jail. Sala Malekun, Malekun Sala.*

(Say the name of the new initiate), *May you never be in front of a judge against you. Sala Malekun, Malekun Sala.*

(Say the name of the new initiate), *May you always be victorious over all of your enemies known and unknown. Sala Malekun, Malekun Sala.*

(Say the name of the new initiate), *May the spirits always give you light in darkness. Sala Malekun, Malekun Sala.*

(Say the name of the new initiate), *May there never be any tragedy in your path. Sala Malekun, Malekun Sala.*

(Say the name of the new initiate), *May death never be in your path. Sala Malekun, Malekun Sala.*

(Say the name of the new initiate), *May illness never be in your path. Sala Malekun, Malekun Sala.*

(Say the name of the new initiate), *May you never be shot. Sala Malekun, Malekun Sala.*

(Say the name of the new initiate), *May you never be stabbed. Sala Malekun, Malekun Sala.*

(Say the name of the new initiate), *May you always avoid the spirit of death. Sala Malekun, Malekun Sala.*

(Say the name of the new initiate), *May the blood that spills today from your body be the only blood that ever spills from your body. Sala Malekun, Malekun Sala.*

(Say the name of the new initiate), *May it be better that your blood spill here tonight in front of the Congo Spirits then it spill in the streets by some tragedy or some accident. Sala Malekun, Malekun Sala.*

(Say the name of the new initiate), *May this be the only blood that ever spills from your body.Sala Malekun, Malekun Sala.*

(Say the name of the new initiate), *May your blood give the spirits new life as they promise that they will give you new life. Sala Malekun, Malekun Sala.*

(Say the name of the new initiate), *May the spirits give you the ability like the deer to leap over your enemies. Sala Malekun, Malekun Sala.*

(Say the name of the new initiate), *May your enemies not see nor hear this ceremony here tonight. Sala Malekun, Malekun Sala.*

Using a new razor blade, the Ozainista Priest will then proceed in doing the Ozain Initiation Ceremony by cutting the skin of the new initiate. As the Ozainista Priest makes the cuts in the skin on the new initiate, he will rub the specially prepared powder called "*Polvo De Muerto*" directly into the cuts of the new initiate. As the Ozainista Priest rubs the powder into the cuts of the new initiate, the wax from the white candle that was lighted at the beginning of the ceremony will be poured directly on top of the areas where the initiation cuts were done.The magical powder used in this ceremony to place into the "scratching" is different from the powder used in the Rayado Initiation Ceremony.

THE OZAIN INITIATION RAYADO SCRATCHINGS "CUTS" ARE DONE ON ALL OF THE FOLLOWING PLACES ON THE NEW INITI-ATES BODY: (BOTH SIDES OF THE UPPER TORSO, ON BOTH HANDS, ON BOTH SIDES OF THE BACK UPPER TORSO, ON THE BACK OF BOTH LEGS).THIS IS THE CORRECT WAY TO RITUALLY GIVE AND TO PRESENT THE OZAIN INITIATION RAYADO MARKINGS. THE MARKINGS "CUTS" SHOULD NOT BE MORE THAN 1 INCH IN LENGTH. IF THE CEREMONY IS DONE CORRECTLY, THE MARKINGS WILL USUALLY HEAL BEFORE THE NEXT MORNING OR BEFORE 24 HOURS AFTER THE RITUAL OZAIN INITIATION CEREMONY. WHEN THE CUTS HAVE BEEN COMPLETELY SEALED WITH THE WHITE CANDLE WAX, THE TATA WILL SPIRITUALLY SEAL EACH OF THE OZAIN INITIATION RAYADO AREAS BY PRESSING THE MIRRORED END OF THE MPAKA OF OZAIN (GURUNFINDA) AGAINST THE NEWLY CUT AREAS (STAMPING). AFTERWARDS, THE TATA WILL TELL THE NEW INITIATE TO OPEN THEIR MOUTH. WHEN THE NEW INITIATE OPENS THEIR MOUTH, THE CANDLE FLAME IS EXTINGUISHED DIRECTLY ON THE NEW INITIATE'S TONGUE.

24. The individual will dress themselves in all white clothes.

25. The "Fundamento of Ozain" will be left completely underground for nine days and nine nights.

26. At the end of the nine days and nine nights, all of the items will be unearthed and fed the blood of the following animals; Two black roosters, a water turtle and a guinea hen.

27. After feeding the spirit, take the new initiate to the river.

28. Draw the "*Fundameto symbol*" of the spirit Ozain using cascarilla on the flat ground.

29. Place the "*Fundamento of Ozain*" into the center of the symbol.

30. Place a white candle in each of the cardinal directions surrounding the "*Fundamento of Ozain*".

31. Offer cigar smoke and rum to the spirits.

32. Sacrifice two black roosters and a water turtle to the Congo Spirit Ozain and then pour bee's honey over all of the items.

33. The bodies of the animals should be placed to one side of the river ritual area.

34. Using the four coconut shell Chamalongo divination method, check to see if the offerings were accepted with blessings.

35. The Ozain along with the others items should be taken back to the temple where it will be fed the blood of a rooster for nine consecutive Fridays.

36. After the ninth Friday, take the "*Fundamento of Ozain*" to the river and wash the outside of the clay dish with the water.

THE "FUNDAMENTO OF OZAIN" SHOULD ALWAYS HAVE A LIGHTED CANDLE NEXT TO IT. THIS SPIRIT SHOULD BE KEPT IN A DARK LOCATION IN YOUR TEMPLE.

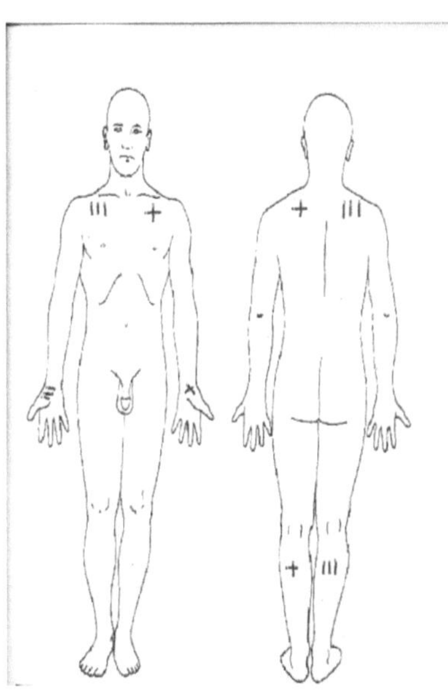

A DIAGRAM SHOWING THE PLACES WHERE THE RAYADO MARKS MUST GO. THIS DIAGRAM CAN ALSO BE USED TO DETERMINE WHERE THE MARKS GO WHEN AN INDIVIDUAL RECEIVES OZAIN. THESE MARKS MAY DIFFER FROM MUNANZO TO MUNANZO.

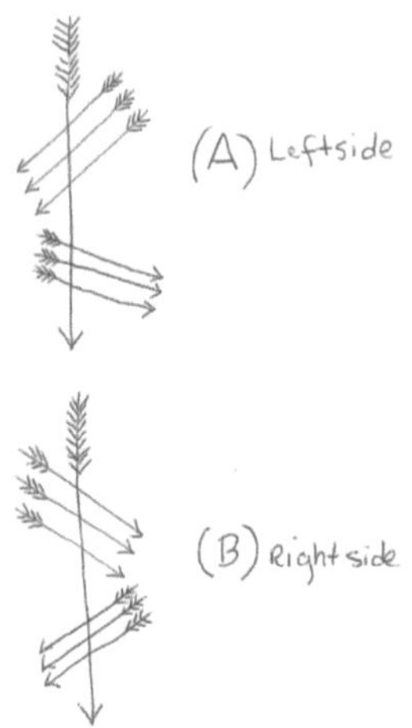

THE ABOVE MARKS ARE USED FOR THE OZAIN INITIATION RITUAL.

HOW TO MAKE CHAMBA DE OZAIN

The sacred drink made and used by all Ozainista Priests on the *Good Friday* religious celebration is called "*Chamba De Ozain*". This very powerful and magical drink is used by an Ozainista Priest during this very important religious celebration. This secret formulated magical drink gives the Ozainista Priest supernatural healing and magical occult powers. This drink contains the powerful and magical essence of the Congo Spirit Ozain.

CHAMBA INGREDIENTS

DIRT FROM 121 TOMBS, DIRT FROM 121 DIFFERENT LOCATIONS, HUMAN BONE POWDER FROM A MAN, 121 POWDERED HERBS, 121 POWDERED PALOS, DEER HORN POWDER, POWDERED ACHE DE SANTO HERB, A VARIETY OF VARIOUS DIFFERENT TYPES OF RED CHILIES, 121 HERB OMIERO, FRESH CEIBA TREE LEAFS, DIRT FROM THE CROSSROADS, RUM (AGUARDIENTE), BLOOD FROM A WATER TURTLE.

CHAMBA INSTRUCTIONS

1. USING A MORTAR AND PESTLE, GRIND ALL OF THE DIRTS INTO A FINE POWDER.

2. PLACE ABOUT A TABLESPOON OF THE POWDERED DIRTS INTO AN EMPTY LIQUOR BOTTLE.

3. PLACE THE POWDERED HUMAN BONE POWDER, POWDERED PALOS INTO THE EMPTY LIQUOR BOTTLE.

4. PLACE ABOUT A HANDFUL OF FRESH CEIBA LEAFS INTO THE BOTTLE.

5. ADD ALL OF THE RED CHILES INTO THE EMPTY BOTTLE.

6. AFTER ALL OF THE INGREDIENTS HAVE BEEN PLACED INTO THE BOTTLE FILL IT UP TO THE RIM WITH THE LIQUOR.

AFTER THE 21 DAYS, THE ***CHAMBA DE OZAIN*** *WILL BE READY TO USE.*

HOW TO PREPARE THE SACRED POWDER OF OZAIN

The Following sacred formula is how to correctly prepare the sacred "*Ozain Initiation Powder*" used in the initiation ceremony of the "*Fundamento of Ozain*". This sacred powder may be prepared in a different manner depending on the Congo religious system which you are being initiated into. If you received your Ozain Initiation Ceremony and the Ozainista Priest did not place this sacred *Ozain Rayado Initiation Powder* into the "*Rayado* scratchings" your Ozain Initiation Ceremony was not done correctly. It is only by placing this sacred powder into your "*Ozain Rayado scratchings*" that the new initiate will be spiritually connected to the Congo Spirit of Ozain. If you did not have this done during your Ozain Initiation Ceremony, the Congo Spirit Ozain will not be able to protect you nor will he be able to recognize you as one of his own children. This sacred powder is also referred to as "*Polvo De Ozain*" or *Afoche* by the initiates of Caribbean Palo Mayombe religious tradition.

INGREDIENTS NECESSARY

DIRT FROM 121 TOMBS

DIRT FROM 121 DIFFERENT LOCATIONS

HUMAN BONE POWDER FROM 21 DIFFERENT MEN

POWDERED BONE FROM 21 BIRDS OF FLIGHT

121 POWDERED HERBS

121 POWDERED PALOS

DEER HORN POWDER

POWDERED BONE FROM A WOLF or LION or COYOTE

POWDERED ACHE DE SANTO HERB (OPTIONAL)

HOW TO MAKE THE SACRED SPIRIT OMIERO

The sacred herbal liquid drink of the spirits is known as omiero. Omiero is a specially prepared drink which is believed to have magical properties. Every spirit has their own sacred omiero attributed to them.

Omiero is prepared with a variety of ingredients such as rain water, sea water, palm oil, cascarilla, honey and a variety of herbs. Omiero is used in all of the ceremonies and rituals. Omiero is used for such things as to consecrate the sacred beads (collares), chamalongo divination shells, amulets and to feed the matarib sacred spirit stones). Omiero is also used by initiates as medicine. Omiero has been known to heal disease and spiritual sickness.

The number of fresh herbs used in the preparation of the omiero depends on the particular spirit being invokes and prepared. The following is a chart for the number of herbs attributed to each of the major Congo Spirit deities.

GENERAL OMIERO *- 21 OR 121 HERBS*

LUCERO OMIERO *- 21 OR 121 HERBS*

EGGUN OMIERO *- 9, 21 OR 121 HERBS*

CENTELLE NDOKI OMIERO *- 9 HERBS*

ZARABANDA OMIERO *- 9 HERBS*

TIEMBLA TIERRA OMIERO *- 8 HERBS*

MADRE DE AGUA OMIERO *- 7 HERBS*

MAMA SHOLAN OMIERO *- 5 HERBS*

CABO RONDO OMIERO *- 7 HERBS*

PRENDA JUDIA OMIERO - 9, *21, 121 HERBS*

OZAIN OMIERO - *21 OR 121 HERBS*

BRAZO FUERTE OMIERO - *6 HERBS*

SIETE RAYOS OMIERO - *6 or 7 HERBS*

KOBAYENDE OMIERO - *16 HERBS*

NSAMBA NTALA OMIERO - *2, 4 OR 21 HERBS*

AJE SPIRITS OMIERO - *9, 21 OR 121 HERBS*

ITEMS NECESSARY TO PREPARE THE OMIERO

1. *ONE LARGE BOWL*
2. *TWENTY-ONE GRAINS OF PARADISE*
3. *BEE'S HONEY*
4. *POWDERED SMOKED FISH*
5. *POWDERED SMOKED JUTIA*
6. *CIGARS*
7. *RUM*
8. *(4) PIECES OF PREPARED COCONUTS FOR DIVINATION*
9. *ONE STRAW MAT (ESTERA)*
10. *PEMBA*
11. *FRESH HERBS*
12. *FRESH WATER*
13. *HOLY WATER*
14. *MAY RAIN WATER*
15. *COCONUT WATER*

(HOLY WATER FROM A CHURCH IS OPTIONAL)

PREPARATION

1. Lay the straw mat on the floor.

2. Place the large bowl which you will be preparing the Omiero into the center of the straw mat.

3. Pour all of the waters into the bowl.

4. Place all of the herbs on the mat.

5. Spray the herbs with rum and blow the smoke from a cigar over all of the herbs.

6. Place all of the items which you will be using to prepare the omiero on the mat.

7. Light a white candle and place it next to the bowl.

8. Pick up all of the herbs in both of your hands and hold them up to the sky and say and do the following:

CON LA BENDICION Y LA LICENCIA DE NSAMBI,

SALA MALEKUN, MALEKUN SALA

CON LA BENDICION Y LA LICENCIA DE EGGUN,

SALA MALEKUN, MALEKUN SALA

CON LA BENDICION Y LA LICENCIA DE LUCERO - SALA MALEKUN, MALEKUN SALA

CON LA BENDICION Y LA LICENCIA DE OZAIN - SALA MALEKUN, MALEKUN SALA

CON LA BENDICION Y LA LICENCIA DE - SAY THE NAME OF THE SPIRIT - SALA MALEKUN, MALEKUN SALA

9. After saying the above prayer, kiss the herbs in your hands three times and then begin to pull off all of the leaves and place them into the bowl.

10. Sitting in a chair in front of the bowl, begin ripping and tearing the herbs in the waters. This is called making *"Ozain."*

11. Sing the following mambo while making the omiero:

KAMA MA IYA - IYA IYA
KAMA MA ENU - ENU ENU
KAMA MA EBO - EBO EBO
KAMA MA EBO - EBO EBO
MA MA MA IYA IYA IYA.
MA MA MA IYA IYA IYA.
MA MA MA IYA IYA IYA.
EBO EBO EBO EBO EBO
EBO EBO EBO EBO EBO
EWE EWE EWE EWE EWE
EWE EWE EWE EWE EWE
MA MA MA IYA IYA IYA.
MA MA MA IYA IYA IYA.
MA MA MA IYA IYA IYA.
EBO EBO EBO EBO EBO
EBO EBO EBO EBO EBO
EWE EWE EWE EWE EWE
EWE EWE EWE EWE EWE

REPEAT THIS SONG UNTIL YOU HAVE FINISHED PREPARING THE OMIERO.

12. When you have finished, add the following items into the omiero liquid; honey, grains of paradise, smoked fish and jutia.

13. Check with the four coconut pieces in the divination ritual to see if the omiero has been prepared correctly.

14. If the answer comes with a yes then drip candle wax into the omiero liquid. The amount of drops will depend on the spirit omiero being prepared. Use the chart on the first page of this chapter. (For example if the omiero is for the Spirit Zarabanda then place 9 drops of candle wax into the omiero)

THE CANDLE WAX SEALS THE MAGICAL POWER (ACHE) OF HERBS INTO THE SACRED OMIERO.

HOW TO DO A ROMPEMIENTO SPIRITUAL CLEANSING

The Spanish word, "rompemiento" means to "tearoff" or to "break". A rompemiento spiritual cleansing is done on an individual to cleanse them of negative vibrations. It is the most common spiritual cleansing ritual done by Congo Priests. The following rompemiento cleansing ceremony is done at the river, but it can be done anywhere that is determined by the spirits.

1. *Light a white candle and present it to the following areas of the individual; top of head, their feet, their left shoulder, there right shoulder, the top of the head once again, the ground at the back of the feet, the left shoulder, the right shoulder.*

2. *Afterwards, give the candle to the individual in their hands and ask them to pray silently to Nzambi, to their ancestors and to the Congo spirits for blessings.*

3. *Light a cigar and blow the smoke over the body of the individual. (3 times). Take a mouthful of rum and blow it over the body of the individual. (3 times)*

4. *After the individual has finished praying, take the white candle and stick it into the ground.*

5. *Take a black hen/black rooster and spiritually cleanse the individual from head to toe. After, give the black hen/black rooster to the individual and tell them to hold it up to their forehead and pray to their ancestors and to the Congo Spirits to seek their blessings.*

6. *After they have finished praying, ritually sacrifice the bird and feed the blood around the area which the individual is standing.*

7. *Place the body of the bird near the candle and pour bee's honey over it and into the river.*

8. *Begin the Rompemiento by tearing the individuals clothes off and then set the clothes next to the candle. Light a cigar and blow the smoke over the body of the individual. (3 times). Take a mouthful of rum and blow it over the body of the individual. (3 times)*

9. *The individual will then bathe using omiero and will scrub their bodies using 9 fresh herbs. When the individual has finished, assist the individual to place on new white clothes.*

THERE ARE VARIOUS METHODS OF HOW TO DO THIS SPIRITUAL CLEANSING, BUT THIS IS THE BASIC SPIRITUAL INSTRUCTIONS ABOUT HOW TO DO A ROMPEMIENTO SPIRITUAL CLEANSING CORRECTLY.

HOW TO FEED THE EARTH SPIRITUAL CLEANSING

"*DARLE A COMER A LA TIERRA*"

A "*Feeding the Earth*" cleansing ceremony is done on an individual to cleanse them of spiritual sickness and or a bad spiritual energy. The Earth is spiritually fed so that the spirit of death will be satisfied and will not take the individual in a physical death. The following "*Feeding the Earth*" cleansing ceremony rompemiento cleansing can be done anywhere that is determined by the spirits.

1. *Dig a large hole in front of the individual who will be receiving the spiritual cleansing about 2 feet deep.*

2. *Light a cigar and blow the smoke over the entire body of the individual who is receiving the spiritual cleansing.*

3. *Take a mouthful of rum and blow it over the entire body of the individual who is receiving the spiritual cleansing.*

4. *The individual who is receiving the spiritual cleansing will then clean themselves with a mixture of (21) different types of dry grains (rice, beans, oatmeal, etc.). The individual cleans themselves by grabbing a large amount of the (21) different grains in both of their hands and holds their fists tightly while they themselves are rubbing their entire body from head to toe.*

5. *As the individual finishes spiritually cleaning themselves using the (21) grains they will throw the grains into the hole directly in front of them.*

6. *The individual cleanses themselves with the grains until all of the grains are in the hole.*

7. *The Congo Priest will then cleanse the individual using a black rooster or a black hen.*

8. *After the Congo Priest has finished cleaning the individual with the bird, they then give it to the individual who is receiving the cleansing to hold it.*

9. *The individual then holds the bird up to their forehead and then prays to Nzambi, the spirits and to their Eggun to remove any obstacles from their path.*

10. *After the individual has finished praying, they then give the bird back to the Congo Priest who then prays to the spirit of the Earth to take away any evil and obstacles from the individual in exchange for the sacrifice and blood of the bird.*

11. *After the Congo Priest has finished praying then they will sacrifice the bird and allow the blood of the bird to feed to ground area around the individual and also into the hole.*

12. *The Congo Priest then throws the bird into the hole and pours bee's honey over it.*

13. *The Congo Priest will then do a Rompemiento spiritual cleansing on the individual by tearing off their clothes and then throwing the clothes into the hole.*

14. *The Congo Priest then blows smoke and rum over the entire body of the individual.*

15. *The individual then takes a spiritual herbal omiero bath made from 21 different herbs while standing directly in front of the hole.*

16. *After the individual has finished taking the spiritual bath the Congo Priest then pours the remaining bath into the hole.*

17. *The individual then puts on their new white clothes while the Congo Priest covers the hole completely using dirt by forming a mound over the hole.*

18. *The Congo Priest will then give a lighted red candle to the individual to pray over it,*

19. *After the individual prays over the candle they will then place it into the center of the dirt mound to remain there until it has finished burning.*

20. *After the individual places the candle into the dirt mound, the individual and the Congo Priest will then depart from the area and to never return there.*

THIS IS THE AUTHENTIC WAY TO TRADITIONALLY FEED THE EARTH FOR AN INDIVIDUAL. THIS POWERFUL SPIRITUAL CLEANSING IS DONE TO REMOVE A BAD SPIRIT FROM AROUND THE INDIVIDUAL, TO REMOVE WITCHCRAFT AND ALSO TO REMOVE SPIRITUAL SICKNESS. THIS SPIRITUAL CLEANSING CAN SAVE THE LIFE OF THE INDIVIDUAL. THIS SPIRITUAL CLEANSING SHOULD BE DONE AWAY FROM THE CONGO MUNANZO AT THE MOUNTAINS, FIELD OR IN A FOREST.

CEMETERY RITUALS OF OZAIN

A cemetery ritual usually is done to remove a bad spirit or black magic from an individual.

ITEMS NECESSARY

ONE ROOSTER
FOUR BLACK CANDLES
HONEY
RED WINE
RUM
CIGAR
PEMBA

1. *Dig a large hole in the ground at the base of a large tree.*

2. *Using pemba, draw the Ozain spirit signature of the CEMETERY RITUAL around the large hole. The hole will be directly in the center of the Ozain spirit signature.*

3. *Place the "Mpaka of Ozain" next to the hole.*

4. *Place the four white candles in all of the cardinal directions (North, South, East, West), around the hole.*

5. *Light the candles.*

6. *Light the cigar and blow the smoke over the ritual area and directly into the hole.*

7. *Take a mouthful of rum and blow it over the ritual area and directly into the hole.*

8. *Invoke the Congo Spirit Ozain using the general ritual prayer.*

9. *Cleanse yourself and the others who are present there with the rooster.*

10. *When you have finished, ritually sacrifice the rooster and allow the blood to drip directly into the hole and over the Mpaka of Ozain.*

11. *When the rooster is dead, place the body into the hole.*

12. *Pour honey over the body in the hole.*

13. *Wash your hands and the knife using fresh water and rum directly over the hole.*

14. *Pour red wine into the hole.*

15. *Using the four coconut shell chamalongo divination method, check to see if the offerings were accepted with blessings of the spirits.*

16. *If the spirits respond positive, cover the hole up with dirt and allow the candles to remain burning until completely finished.*

17. *Leave the area and don't look back.*

FOREST RITUALS OF OZAIN

A Forest ritual usually is done to open up the roads to success for an individual who is having bad luck.

INGREDIENTS NECESSARY

ONE PIGEON
FOUR WHITE CANDLES
HONEY
RED WINE
RUM
CIGAR
PEMBA

1. *Dig a large hole in the ground at the base of a large tree.*

2. *Using pemba, draw the Ozain spirit signature of the FOREST RITUAL around the large hole. The hole will be directly in the center of the Ozain spirit signature.*

3. *Place the "Mpaka of Ozain" next to the hole.*

4. *Place the four white candles in all of the cardinal directions (North, South, East, West), around the hole.*

5. *Light the candles.*

6. *Light the cigar and blow the smoke over the ritual area and directly into the hole.*

7. *Take a mouthful of rum and blow it over the ritual area and directly into the hole.*

8. *Invoke the Congo Spirit Ozain using the general ritual prayer.*

9. *Cleanse yourself and the others who are present there with the pigeon.*

10. *When you have finished, ritually sacrifice the pigeon and allow the blood to drip directly into the hole and over the Mpaka of Ozain.*

11. *When the pigeon is dead, place the body into the hole.*

12. *Pour honey over the body in the hole.*

13. *Wash your hands and the knife using fresh water and rum directly over the hole.*

14. *Pour red wine into the hole.*

15. *Using the four coconut shell chamalongo divination method, check to see if the offerings were accepted with blessings of the spirits.*

16. *If the spirits respond positive, cover the hole up with dirt and allow the candles to remain burning until completely finished.*

17. *Leave the area and don't look back.*

RAILROAD RITUALS OF OZAIN

A Railroad ritual usually is done to remove black magic and to remove legal problems from around an individual.

ITEMS NECESSARY

ONE BLACK ROOSTER
TWO BLACK CANDLES & TWO GREEN CANDLES
HONEY
BEER
RED WINE
RUM
CIGAR
PEMBA

1. *Dig a large hole in the ground at the base of a large tree.*

2. *Using pemba, draw the Ozain spirit signature of the RAILROAD RITUAL around the large hole. The hole will be directly in the center of the Ozain spirit signature.*

3. *Place the "Mpaka of Ozain" next to the hole.*

4. *Place the four white candles in all of the cardinal directions (North, South, East, West), around the hole.*

5. *Light the candles.*

6. *Light the cigar and blow the smoke over the ritual area and directly into the hole.*

7. *Take a mouthful of rum and blow it over the ritual area and directly into the hole.*

8. *Invoke the Congo Spirit Ozain using the general ritual prayer.*

9. *Cleanse yourself and the others who are present there with the rooster.*

10. *When you have finished, ritually sacrifice the rooster and allow the blood to drip directly into the hole and over the Mpaka of Ozain.*

11. *When the rooster is dead, place the body into the hole.*

12. *Pour honey over the body in the hole.*

13. *Wash your hands and the knife using fresh water and rum directly over the hole.*

14. *Pour red wine into the hole.*

15. *Using the four coconut shell chamalongo divination method, check to see if the offerings were accepted with blessings of the spirits.*

16. *If the spirits respond positive, cover the hole up with dirt and allow the candles to remain burning until completely finished.*

17. *Leave the area and don't look back.*

RIVER RITUALS OF OZAIN

A River ritual usually is done to remove any obstacles that are stopping or preventing an individual from attracting love, romance or a marriage partner.

ITEMS NECESSARY

ONE BROWN HEN
FOUR YELLOW CANDLES
HONEY
PINK CHAMPAGNE
RUM
CIGAR
PEMBA

1. *Dig a large hole in the ground at the base of a large tree.*

2. *Using pemba, draw the Ozain spirit signature of the RIVER RITUAL around the large hole. The hole will be directly in the center of the Ozain spirit signature.*

3. *Place the "Mpaka of Ozain" next to the hole.*

4. *Place the four white candles in all of the cardinal directions (North, South, East, West), around the hole.*

5. *Light the candles.*

6. *Light the cigar and blow the smoke over the ritual area and directly into the hole.*

7. *Take a mouthful of rum and blow it over the ritual area and directly into the hole.*

8. *Invoke the Congo Spirit Ozain using the general ritual prayer.*

9. *Cleanse yourself and the others who are present there with the hen.*

10. *When you have finished, ritually sacrifice the hen and allow the blood to drip directly into the hole and over the Mpaka of Ozain.*

11. *When the hen is dead, place the body into the hole.*

12. *Pour honey over the body in the hole.*

13. *Wash your hands and the knife using fresh water and rum directly over the hole.*

14. *Pour pink champagne into the hole.*

15. *Using the four coconut shell chamalongo divination method, check to see if the offerings were accepted with blessings of the spirits.*

16. *If the spirits respond positive, cover the hole up with dirt and allow the candles to remain burning until completely finished.*

17. *Leave the area and don't look back.*

MOUNTAIN RITUALS OF OZAIN

A mountain ritual usually is done to overcome any and all enemies known and unknown.

ITEMS NECESSARY

ONE PIGEON
FOUR WHITE CANDLES
HONEY
RED WINE
RUM
CIGAR
PEMBA

1. Dig a large hole in the ground at the base of a large tree.

2. Using pemba, draw the Ozain spirit signature of the MOUNTAIN RITUAL around the large hole. The hole will be directly in the center of the Ozain spirit signature.

3. Place the *"Mpaka of Ozain"*next to the hole.

4.Place the four white candles in all of the cardinal directions (North, South, East, West), around the hole.

5. Light the candles.

6. Light the cigar and blow the smoke over the ritual area and directly into the hole.

7. Take a mouthful of rum and blow it over the ritual area and directly into the hole.

8. Invoke the Congo Spirit Ozain using the general ritual prayer.

9. Cleanse yourself and the others who are present there with the rooster.

10. When you have finished, ritually sacrifice the rooster and allow the blood to drip directly into the hole and over the Mpaka of Ozain.

11. When the rooster is dead, place the body into the hole.

12. Pour honey over the body in the hole.

13. Wash your hands and the knife using fresh water and rum directly over the hole.

14. Pour red wine into the hole.

15. Using the four coconut shell chamalongo divination method, check to see if the offerings were accepted with blessings of the spirits.

16. If the spirits respond positive, cover the hole up with dirt and allow the candles to remain burning until completely finished.

17. Leave the area and don’t look back.

FIELD RITUALS OF OZAIN

A Field ritual usually is done to remove spiritual sickness and or disease from an individual.

ITEMS NECESSARY

ONE ROOSTER
FOUR WHITE CANDLES
HONEY
WHITE WINE
MIXED DRY BEANS & RICE
RUM
CIGAR
PEMBA

1. Dig a large hole in the ground at the base of a large tree.

2. Using pemba, draw the Ozain spirit signature of the FIELD RITUAL around the large hole. The hole will be directly in the center of the Ozain spirit signature.

3. Place the *"Mpaka of Ozain"*next to the hole.

4.Place the four white candles in all of the cardinal directions (North, South, East, West), around the hole.

5. Light the candles.

6. Light the cigar and blow the smoke over the ritual area and directly into the hole.

7. Take a mouthful of rum and blow it over the ritual area and directly into the hole.

8. Invoke the Congo Spirit Ozain using the general ritual prayer.

9. Cleanse yourself and the others who are present there with the rooster.

10. When you have finished, ritually sacrifice the rooster and allow the blood to drip directly into the hole and over the Mpaka of Ozain.

11. When the rooster is dead, place the body into the hole.

12. Pour honey over the body in the hole.

13. Wash your hands and the knife using fresh water and rum directly over the hole.

14. Pour white wine into the hole.

15. Using the four coconut shell chamalongo divination method, check to see if the offerings were accepted with blessings of the spirits.

16. If the spirits respond positive, cover the hole up with dirt and allow the candles to remain burning until completely finished.

17. Leave the area and don't look back.

A GENERAL INVOCATION OF THE SPIRIT OZAIN

I, (Say your name), a servant of Nzambi, call upon the Spirit Ozain, the Grand Guardian of the mysteries of nature and all that is seen and unseen to hear my spiritual requests. O Most Glorious Spirit Ozain, who bestows upon man the power of sacred herbal knowledge and the secrets of magic and who delivers us from all of our enemies known and unknown, hear my prayers. O Most Glorious Spirit, Ozain, I invoke your sacred and divine powers to manifest here and to grant my request. Salamalekun, Malekunsala. (Say your spiritual request here).

HOW TO RITUALLY WORK WITH THE SPIRIT OZAIN

1. Draw the particular spirit signature of Ozain that you will be working with directly in front of the Okobelefo (ceramic pot containing the mysteries of Ozain).

2. Place your magical working into the center of the spirit signature of Ozain.

3. Place a candle next to the spiritual working and then light it.

The color of the candle will depend on what type of spiritual request that you are seeking from the spirit Ozain. Light one candle each day that the spiritual working remains infront of the "Fundamento of Ozain" until it is complete.

HOW TO RITUALLY SEND OUT THE SPIRIT OZAIN

1. Draw the particular spirit signature of Ozain that you will be working with directly in front of the Okobelefo (ceramic pot containing the mysteries of Ozain).

2. Lay a machete directly in front of the Okobelefo on the ground.

3. Line the blade of the machete with a thin layer of fula (Gun Powder).

4. State you request by invocating the spirit Ozain with the general invocation prayer.

5. Light a cigar and attach it to the end of a long metal pole and then carefully ignite the fula from the end of the handle of the machete.

The handle of the machete should be touching the Okobelefo of Ozain and the blade of the machete should be pointing outwards away from the "Fundamento of Ozain".

HOW TO PREPARE THE SACRED BEADS OF OZAIN

ITEMS NECESSARY

1. *ONE STRAND OF BEADS MADE FOR THE SPIRIT OZAIN.*
2. *OMIERO OF THE SPIRIT OZAIN*
3. *HONEY*
4. *RUM*
5. *RED WINE*
6. *RED ROOSTER*
7. *ONE WHITE CANDLE*
8. *ONE SEVEN COLORED CANDLE*

PREPARATION

1. Place a large bowl of Omiero in front of the "Fundamento of Ozain".

2. Place the strand of beads sacred to the Spirit Ozain" in the Omiero.

3. Light all the candle and place them next to the bowl.

4. Invoke the spirit.

5. Feed the blood of the rooster to the spirit allowing the blood to drip into the bowl over the spirit beads.

6. Pour honey and red wine over the spirits and into the bowl containing the spirit beads.

7. Allow the beads to soak for a 24 hour period of time. After the 24 hours remove the beads and clean using rum and by blowing cigar smoke over them.

8. Set the beads on the "Fundamento of Ozain" allowing them to become energized with the powerful energy of Ozain before presenting them to an individual.

The colors of the beads of Ozain are multi-colored combinations.

HOW TO PREPARE THE MPAKA OF OZAIN

The Mpaka of the spirit Ozain is an important magical tool for the Ozainista Priest. The mysteries of the Mpaka of the spirit Ozain are prepared inside of the horn of a bull. The Mpaka of the spirit Ozain in itself is a miniature "*Fundamento of Ozain*"which can be transported easily and used in powerful magical rituals and cleansing ceremonies in the mountains or in the forest. The Mpaka of the spirit Ozain is the third eye and the ear of the spirit. When a glass mirror is placed on the open end of the Mpaka of the spirit Ozain to cover the magical ingredients inside of the bull's horn, it is called "*Vititi Mensu*". The Congo word "*Vititi Mensu*" means the "All Seeing Eye". The Mpaka of the spirit Ozain can be set next to the "*Fundamento of Ozain*". The Mpaka of the spirit Ozain is ritually fed at the same time that you feed the spirit Ozain.

ITEMS NECESSARY

1. *One large Meteorite stone.*

2. *One lightning stone.*

3. *One Quartz Crystal*

4. *A small amount of the same powdered ingredients used to prepare the Fundamento of Ozain.*

5. *One large Bull's Horn.*

6. *One tablespoon of liquid Mercury.*

7. *Finger and Toe Nail cuttings and Body Hair from various parts of the body of the individual receiving it.*

8. *One round mirror that fits the opening of the Bull's Horn.*

9. *Fast-Dry cement.*

10. Omiero of the spirit Ozain.

LIVE ANIMALS NEEDED

1. *Two Black Roosters*

PREPARATION

1.In a large mixing bowl, prepare an omiero using the fresh herbs. Use the grains of paradise, ocean water, river water, May rain water and the milk from one coconut in the preparation of the omiero.

2.After you have prepared the omiero, place the bull's horn, the lightning stone, the quartz crystal and the meteorite stone into the omiero mixture to soak and remain for 24 hours.

3.Light a large seven day white religious glass candle and set it next to the bowl of omiero to give light and blessings to the sacred items that will go into the Mpaka.

4. After the 24 hours, remove the bull's horn.

5. Take a mouthful of rum and spray it directly into the empty bull's horn.

6. Light a cigar and blow it directly into the bull's horn.

7. After you have finished this procedure, the bull's horn which will be housing the magical elements of the spirit Ozain has been baptized and is now ready to receive the other sacred items.

8. Pour the mercury into the bottom of the empty bull's horn.

9. In a large bucket, mix all of the powdered ingredients together along with the nails and hair.

10. After you have mixed all of these magical ingredients together, pour in some of the omiero mixture into the bucket containing the magical mixture of ingredients and make a thick paste like mixture.

11. Add a small amount of the past mixture into the empty bull's horn and firmly pack it down.

12. Place the lightening stone into the bull's horn.

13. Add some more of the paste mixture into the bull's horn.

14. Place the quartz crystals into the bull's horn and cover with the paste mixture.

15. Feed the mpaka the blood from one rooster and allow it to remain for 3 hours.

16. After the 3 hours, light a white candle and allow the wax to drip over the top of the bull's horn and to completely cover the open end of it.

17. Place the mirror onto the top of the bull's horn on top of the wax.

18. After the wax has dried with the mirror embedded in it, seal the mirror onto the bull's horn with the fast dry cement with a good area of the mirror showing.

19. After the cement has dried, feed the spirit mpaka again with the blood of the other rooster.

THE OUTSIDE OF THE MPAKA OF THE SPIRIT OZAIN CAN BE DECORATED WITH STRANDS OF BEADS AND COWRIE SHELLS. THE COLORS OF THE BEADS WILL BE MULTI-COLORED IN THE TRADITIONAL PATTERN OF THE SPIRIT OZAIN.

THE “TABLERO DE MUERTO”

Divination by cowrie seashells has been used for thousands of years by African priests to determine the spiritual ailment and destiny of an individual. The shells are believed to be the mouth piece of the spirits which when interpreted will reveal the past, present and the future destiny of an individual. The divination of the shells is known to Congo practitioners as *Vititi Nkobo*. The cowrie shells which are used by a Congo priest belong to the Congo Spirit Lucero, the Keeper of the Crossroads. In the Palo Mayombe religious tradition, seashell divination is also known as the Chamalongo. The word Chamalongo means cemetery. The literal translation of the Chamalongo is the divination by means of the spirits from the cemetery and of the spirit nganga. There are many divination methods used by a priest of the Congo religion such as divining with the use of stones, bones, crystals and other items. The interpretations are a mixture of spirituality, spiritual visions and traditional Congo folklore. There are very few initiated Mayomberos (Congo Priest) who actually know the secrets and the Mysteries of the true chamalongo divination ceremony. This very rare form of divination is rarely seen outside of the Caribbean and Brazil. The chamalongo shells are read on a special divination table which is known as the “*Tablero De Muerto*”, the table of the dead. This specially prepared wood divination table is painted and etched with various sacred symbols of the spirits and of the stars, Heavens and the Earth. An Ozainista Priest can also set their your magical and spiritual workings on top of the “*Tablero De Muerto*” to energize and empower them.

A PICTURE SHOWING THE "TABLERO DE MUERTO"

"Afoche" (Ritually Handmade Magical Powders of the Spirit Ozain) refers to the name that practitioners of the Congo religion call all classes and types of magical powders. Afoche powders are usually a blend of various herbs, dirts and other magical ingredients that are powdered into a fine powder. Afoche powders are ritually prepared using sacred prayers and invocations which bring out the magical properties of the particular magical powder being prepared. Afoche powders can be prepared ritually for a variety of different types of spiritual usages from bringing luck, attracting love and for black magic spells of harm and destruction. All of the following Afoche De Ozain powders should be prepared and ritually empowered on top of the "*Tablero De Muerto*" by an Ozainista Priest. These very powerful magical powders can be used by themselves or in combination with any type of magical ritual/spiritual work that you may be doing for yourself or for your other individuals. These magical powders consecrated to the Congo Spirit Ozain are powerful and really do work fast & quick. After the magical Congo ritual of the Spirit Ozain is invoked and the Ozainista Priest has completed making the Afoche Powder, the magic powder should be left on top of the "*Tablero De Muerto*" from 3 to 21 days directly in front of the Spirit Ozain before it can be successfully used in your magical rituals. Although there are various methods of how to prepare these very powerful magical powders, the following is an example of how to prepare them using the "*Tablero De Muerto*" and a few authentic formulas for making these magical Afoche powders of Ozain. All of the magical herbs used in making the magical Afoche of Ozain can be purchased from any well-stocked Botanica or Occult Supply Store.

HOW TO RITUALLY PREPARE AFOCHE POWDERS

All of the following magical powders can be made using the following ritual instructions.

1.*Grind all of the dry herbs listed into a fine powder using a mortal and pestle or an electric coffee bean grinder.*

2.*Mix all of the powdered dry herbs and the other sacred ingredients listed in the Afoche formula together and place into a bowl.*

3.*Place the bowl containing the sacred powder (Afoche powder) in front of the "Fundamento of spirit Ozain". If you do not have the "Fundamento of Ozain" then place the bowl directly on top of the "Tablero De Muerto".*

4.*Light a white candle to the spirit Ozain to empower the magical Afoche powder.*

5.*Say the general invocation prayer of the spirit Ozain and make a spiritual petition of what you want the magical Afoche powder to do.*

6.*Allow the magical Afoche powder to remain until the candle burns completely out.*

7.*After the candle has completely burned out then place the magical Afoche powder in a container until ready to use.*

IF YOU HAVE THE "*FUNDAMENTO OF THE SPIRIT OZAIN*", THEN YOU SHOULD KEEP THE MAGICAL AFOCHE POWDER NEXT TO IT UNTIL READY TO USE. BY KEEPING THE MAGICAL AFOCHE POWDER NEXT TO THE FUNDAMENTO OF OZAIN IT WILL CONTINUE TO BECOME STRONGER AND MORE POWERFUL.

MAGICAL AFOCHE POWDER FORMULAS

CONFLICT AFOCHE POWDER

This particular Afoche is used to cause confict between people or to bring problems to a home.

Palo Malambo, Pica Pica herb, Palo Cambia Rumbo, Black Pepper seeds, Spider powder, Scorpion powder.

SEPARATION AFOCHE POWDER

This particular Afoche is used to bring problems between two people to cause a separation of the relationship.

Palo Cambia Voz, Yo Puedo Mas Que Tu herb, Palo Cambia Rumbo, Semillas de Maravilla Roja herb, Black Pepper seeds, Hydrangea Flowers, Dirt from 9 Tombs, Dirt from an Ant Hill, Human Bone Powder, powdered Bat, Powdered Snake.

COME TO ME AFOCHE POWDER

This particular Afoche is used to bring a desired individual to you.

Amansa Guapo herb, Para Mi herb, Patchouli herb,Boton De Oro herb, Orange rind, Corriander seeds, Lemon Grass, Patchouli herb, Dill seed.

FAST LUCK AFOCHE POWDER

This particular Afoche is used to bring luck and success to an individual.

Abre Camino herb, Para Mi herb, Paraiso herb, Palo Arrasa Con Todo, Mint herb,Verbena herb, Nutmeg herb, Five Finger Grass herb, Devil's Shoestring herb.

DOMINATION AFOCHE POWDER

This particular Afoche is used to dominate an individual or to control a situation.

Palo Vence Batalla, Dormidera herb, Flax seeds,Rosemary herb, High John the Conqueror root, Red Chilie Pepper powder.

ESCAPE THE LAW AFOCHE POWDER

This particular Afoche is used to escape the law or to get away from legal problems.

Abre Camino herb, Vencedor herb, Salvia herb, Yo Puedo Mas Que Tu herb, Anise seeds, Fennel seeds, Deer horn powder, Guinea hen eggshell powder, Dirt from 12 Noon, Dirt from 12 Midnight, Powdered Coyote bones.

COURT VICTORY AFOCHE POWDER

This particular Afoche is used to bring a court victory to an individual has legal problems.

Palo Alamo, Vencedor herb,Lengua De Vaca herb,Siempre Viva herb, Sauco Blanco herb,Salvia herb, Dirt from a Court, Chameleon Lizard powder, Deerhorn powder.

REVERSIBLE AFOCHE POWDER

This particular Afoche is used to reverse a negative situation or to banish away problems.

Vencedor herb, Salvadera herb,Rompe Zaraguey herb,Bay Leaf herb, Helencho herb,Camphor Tree leaf, Chameleon Lizard powder.

ROAD CLOSE AFOCHE POWDER

This particular Afoche is used to reverse a negative situation or to banish away problems.

Palo Cambia Voz, Ceiba tree herb, Dirt from 9 Tombs, Dirt from the Crossroads, Dirt from an Alley way, Dirt from the Gate of a Cemetery.

ROAD OPENER AFOCHE POWDER

This particular Afoche is used to open up your roads and to bring success to any situation.

Abre Camino herb, Mejorana herb,Galangal root, Five Finger Grass herb, Basil herb, Mint herb, Vencedor herb, Palo Para Mi, Deer Horn powder, Irosun powder.

HEX BREAKER AFOCHE POWDER

This particular Afoche is used to reverse a negative situation or to banish away a hex which was placed against you.

Vencedor herb,Palo Flamboyan, Espanta Muerto herb, Anamu herb, Palo Quita Maldicion, Rompe Camisa herb, Vence Guerra herb, Cascarilla powder, Black Mustard seeds, Palo Alamo, Irosun powder.

LOVE & ATTRACTION AFOCHE POWDER

This particular Afoche is used to attract love and romance to an individual.

Abre Camino herb, Vencedor herb, Para Mi herb, the Purple Flower from the Campana tree. Cundiamor herb, Damiana herb, Jezebel root, Lovage root, Patchouli herb,Lavender Flowers,

THINK OF ME ALWAYS AFOCHE POWDER

This particular Afoche is used to make individuals think of you all the time.

Para Mi herb, Amansa Guapo herb,Basil herb,No Mi Olvides herb, Catnip herb, Sensitiva herb.

DESTROYER AFOCHE POWDER

This particular Afoche is used to destroy and individual or to brings problems to them

Palo Flamboyan, Palo Papaya, Palo Tumba y Desbaratar, Palo Muerto, Palo Cambia Rumba, Human Bone Powder, Dirt from 9 Tombs of Men, Hair from a Dog & Cat, Dirt from the Crossroads, Powdered Crab Shell.

HOW TO PREPARE A TALISMAN OF THE SPIRIT OZAIN

The magical talismans or amulets that an Ozainista Priest makes are called *Niche Ozain*. These amulets or talismans are also called in the Spanish language, *Resguardos* (Spirit Guards). After the Ozainsita Priest makes the Niche Ozain they are soaked in the sacred liquid omiero and ritually consecrated for the particular Congo spirit.The *Niche Ozain* talisman can be carried in the pocket or purse of an individual. The following are formulas of how to prepare a specific type of *Niche Ozain* talisman that spiritually walks with the Congo spirits.

INSTRUCTIONS FOR PREPARING THE NICHE OZAIN

1. Place all of the sacred ingredients into a small hollow goat's horn. The goat's horn should be no more than 2 to 4 inches in length.

2. After placing all of the sacred ingredients into the goat's horn by firmly packing them into it very tightly then seal closed the end of the horn using fast-dry cement.

3. After sealing in the sacred ingredients into the goat's horn using the fast-dry cement then place a cowrie shell into the fast-dry cement with the mouth of the cowrie shell facing outwards.

4. After the *Niche Ozain* talisman has completely dried then soak it in the sacred liquid omiero for a 24 hour period of time.

5. Place a candle next to the bowl containing the *Niche Ozain* talisman and light it.

6. Say a general prayer to the spirit Ozain and ask him to empower the *Niche Ozain* talisman for what you desire.

7. After the 24 hours then remove the *Niche Ozain* talisman and consecrate it by blowing tabacco smoke over it and by spraying rum over it, 3 times.

8. The *Niche Ozain* talisman is ready to use after it has compelety dried.

9. If you have the "*Fundamento of Ozain*" then you can also ritually feed it with blood.

The Niche Ozain talisman can also be decorated with a strand of beads sacred to the particular Congo spirit that you are preparing it for.

NICHE OZAIN OF THE SPIRIT LUCERO

This particular *Niche Ozain* is used to open up your roads and to bring success to any situation.

Sacred Ingredients: Lightning Stone, Quartz Crystal, Gold, Silver, Dirt from 21 Crossroads, Human Bone Powder, 3 sacred dry herbs of the Orisha Elegua, Peonia seed.

Sacred Omiero: 3 sacred fresh herbs of the *Orisha Elegua*.

NICHE OZAIN OF THE SPIRIT ZARABANDA

This particular *Niche Ozain* is used to protect an individual against witchcraft and against accidents.

Sacred Ingredients: Lightning Stone, Quartz Crystal, Gold, Silver, Dirt from a Railroad Crossing, Human Bone Powder, 7 sacred dry herbs of the Orisha Ogun, Peonia seed.

Sacred Omiero: 7 sacred fresh herbs of the *Orisha Ogun*.

NICHE OZAIN OF THE SPIRIT SIETE RAYOS

This particular *Niche Ozain* is used for protection and to bring success and wealth to an individual.

Sacred Ingredients: Lightning Stone, Quartz Crystal, Gold, Silver, Dirt from the foot of a Palm Tree, Dirt from a Mountain, Human Bone Powder, 6 sacred dry herbs of the Orisha Shango, Peonia seed.

Sacred Omiero: 6 sacred fresh herbs of the *Orisha Shango.*

NICHE OZAIN OF THE SPIRIT SPIRIT MAMA SHOLAN

This particular *Niche Ozain* is used to attract love and romance to an individual.

Sacred Ingredients: Lightning Stone, Quartz Crystal, Gold, Silver, Sand from the River, Human Bone Powder, 5 sacred dry herbs of the Orisha Oshun, Peonia seed, Magnetic Sand.

Sacred Omiero: 5 sacred fresh herbs of the *Orisha Oshun.*

NICHE OZAIN OF THE SPIRIT MADRE DE AGUA

This particular *Niche Ozain* is used to bring success in matters of infertility.

Sacred Ingredients: Lightning Stone, Quartz Crystal, Gold, Silver, Sand from the Beach, Human Bone Powder, 7 sacred dry herbs of the Orisha Yemaya, Peonia seed, Magnetic Sand.

Sacred Omiero: 7 sacred herbs of the *Orisha Yemaya.*

NICHE OZAIN OF THE SPIRIT CABO RONDO

This particular *Niche Ozain* is used to protect an individual from having any legal problems.

Sacred Ingredients: Lightning Stone, Quartz Crystal, Gold, Silver, Dirt from a Court building, Dirt from a Police Station, Human Bone Powder, 7 sacred dry herbs of the Orisha Ochosi, Peonia seed, Magnetic Sand.

Sacred Omiero: 7 sacred fresh herbs of the *Orisha Ochosi.*

NICHE OZAIN OF THE SPIRIT CENTELLE NDOKI

This particular *Niche Ozain* is used to protect an individual against witchcraft.

Sacred Ingredients: Lightning Stone, Quartz Crystal, Gold, Silver, Dirt from the Gate of a Cemetery, Dirt from 9 Tombs of Women, Human Bone Powder, 9 sacred dry herbs of the Orisha Oya, Peonia seed, Magnetic Sand.

Sacred Omiero: 9 sacred fresh herbs of the *Orisha Oya.*

NICHE OZAIN OF THE SPIRIT TIEMPO VIEJO

This particular *Niche Ozain* is used to bring spiritual balance to an individual.

Sacred Ingredients: Lightning Stone, Quartz Crystal, Gold, Silver, Dirt from a Church, Human Bone Powder, 16 sacred dry herbs of the Orisha Orula, Peonia seed, Magnetic Sand.

Sacred Omiero: 16 sacred fresh herbs of the *Orisha Orula.*

NICHE OZAIN OF THE SPIRIT TIEMBLA TIERRA

This particular *Niche Ozain* is used to protect an individual from going to jail.

Sacred Ingredients: Lightning Stone, Quartz Crystal, Gold, Silver, Dirt from a Jail, Dirt from a Court Building, Human Bone Powder, 8 sacred dry herbs of the Orisha Obatala, Peonia seed, Magnetic Sand.

Sacred Omiero: 8 sacred fresh herbs of the *Orisha Obatala*.

NICHE OZAIN OF THE SPIRIT CALUNGA

This particular *Niche Ozain* is used to bring financial success and money to an individual.

Sacred Ingredients: Lightning Stone, Quartz Crystal, Gold, Silver, Sand from the Ocean, 9 sacred dry herbs of the Orisha Olokun, Peonia seed, Magnetic Sand.

Sacred Omiero: 9 sacred fresh herbs of the *Orisha Olokun*.

NICHE OZAIN OF THE SPIRIT KOBAYENDE

This particular *Niche Ozain* is used to protect an individual against sickness and disease.

Sacred Ingredients: Lightning Stone, Quartz Crystal, Gold, Silver, Dirt from the Forest, Dirt from the Gate of a Cemetery, Human Bone Powder, 17 sacred dry herbs of the Orisha Babaluaye, Peonia seed, Magnetic Sand.

Sacred Omiero: 17 sacred fresh herbs of the *Orisha Babaluaye*.

NICHE OZAIN OF THE SPIRIT BRAZO FUERTE

This particular *Niche Ozain* is used to protect an individual against tragedy.

Sacred Ingredients: Lightning Stone, Quartz Crystal, Lava Rock, Gold, Silver, Dirt from a Mountain, Human Bone Powder, 9 sacred dry herbs of the Orisha Aganyu, Peonia seed, Magnetic Sand,

Sacred Omiero: 9 sacred fresh herbs of the *Orisha Aganyu*.

THE CONGO SPIRIT SIGNATURES

In Congo magic, spirit signature sigils (seals) are symbols connected to a set of ideas by which spirits or deities may be summoned to aware-ness and controlled. The spirit signature sigils connect the spirits to our earthly realm. The spirit signature sigils when used in the appropriate magical manner open up the doors to world of the supernatural. They are used in divinatory practices. In Spanish they are called "Firmas".The spirit signature sigil itself when drawn out on the ground or drawn on an object will call forth the spirit. The spirit signature sigil also serves as a physical focus through which the Congo magician achieves the desired state of mind. Spirit signature sigils represent the secret names of spirits and deities who manifest themselves differently to each magic practitioner. Once the Congo magician has summoned the spirit or deity he may control it, if necessary, by subjecting its sigil to fire or the use of a magical sword or machete. Spirit signature sigils can also serve as amulets, talismans, or meditation tools. Congo spirit signature sigils may be of various signs, such as crosses, tridents, stars associated with different deities. Some of the best spirit sigils are attained through intuition and inspiration. Many come through meditation and the practice of scrying; when a certain pattern seems to appear upon the object which the individual is gazing at. Others believe symbols are occasionally mystically produced when asked for. Congo magicians often times inscribe the spirit signature sigil on ceremonial ritual objects, candles or objects of silver, brass, gold, or glass. Such spirit signatures sigils are considered to be magically powerful. Congo magicians also draw these very sacred and powerful spirit signature sigils directly on the ground in front of the Congo spirit nganga to invoke and to summon the deities to appear and to send them to do their bidding. The following Congo Spirit Signature Sigils (Firmas) of Ozain can be used in rituals or when making a spirit nganga, amulets, macuttos, candles, spells and rituals.

This particular spirit signature of Ozain is used when you are preparing and making the Fundamento of Ozain. This spirit signature is painted on the inside bottom of the Okobelefo.

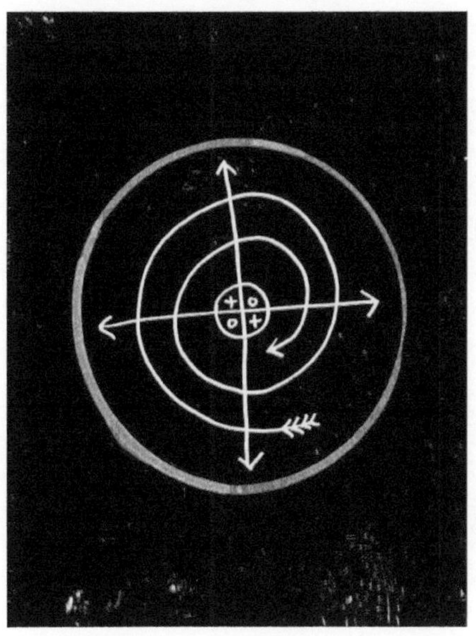

This particular spirit signature of Ozain is used in Cemetery rituals.

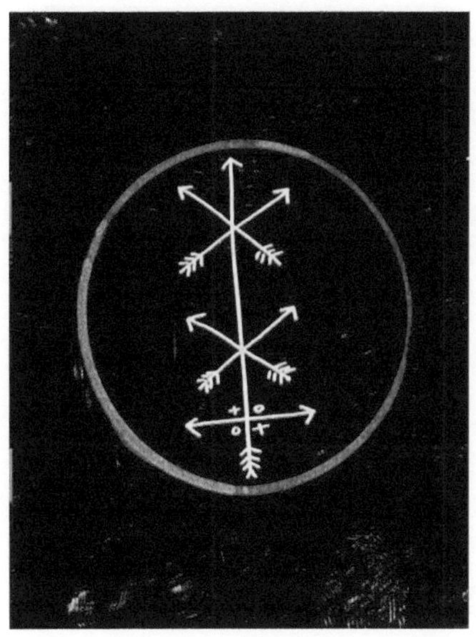

This particular spirit signature of Ozain is used in Forest rituals.

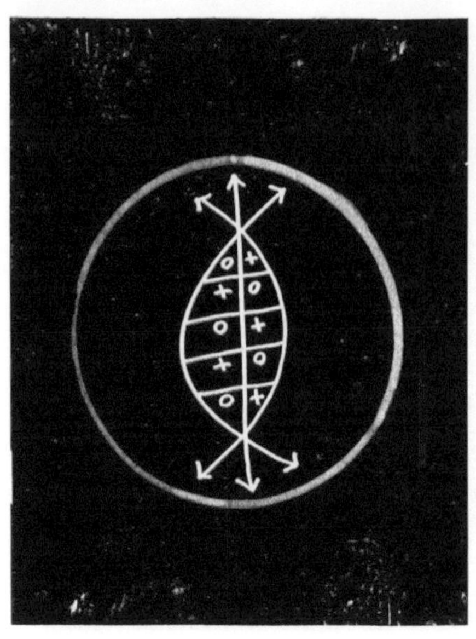

This particular spirit signature of Ozain is used in Railroad rituals.

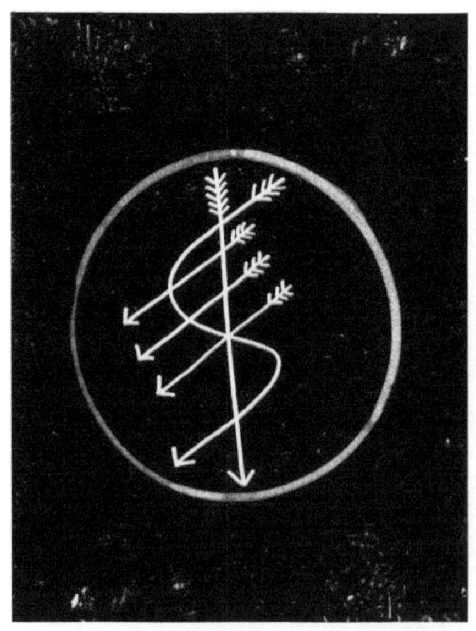

This particular spirit signature of Ozain is used in River rituals.

This particular spirit signature of Ozain is used in Mountain rituals.

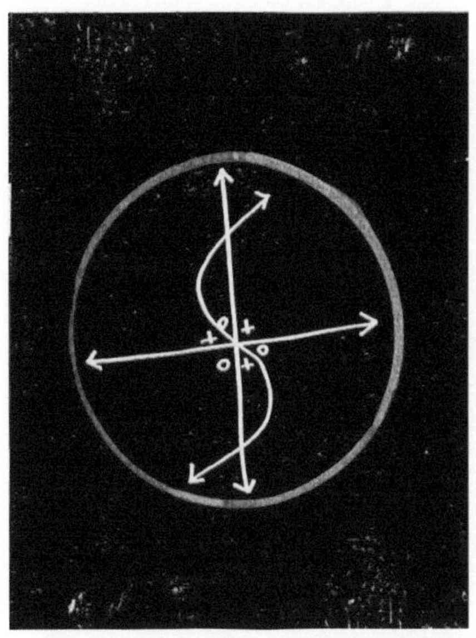

This particular spirit signature of Ozain is used in Field rituals.

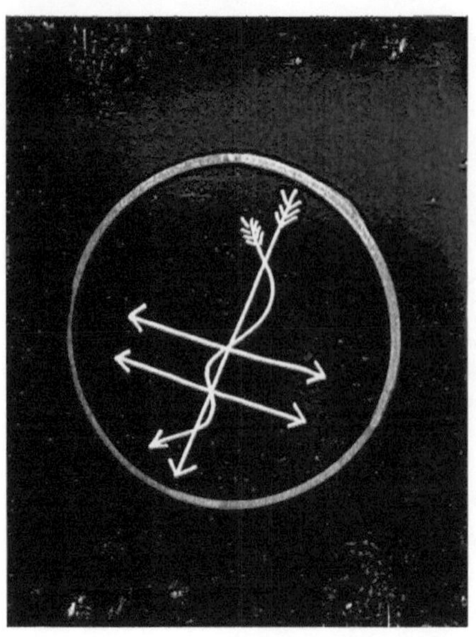

This particular spirit signature of Ozain is used in spells and rituals to banish away bad spirits and negative habits from an individual.

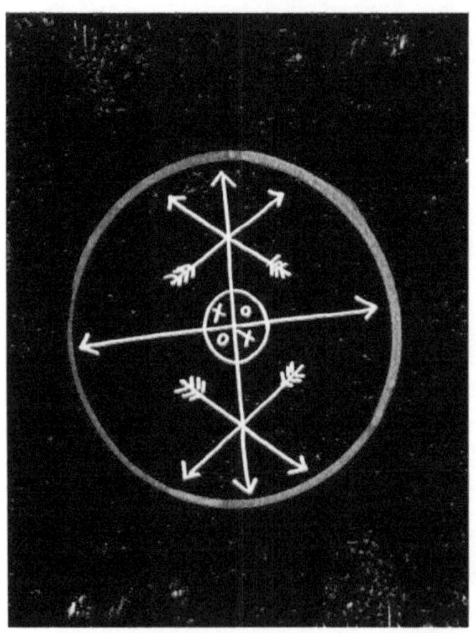

This particular spirit signature of Ozain is used in spells and rituals to hex someone or to close their roads.

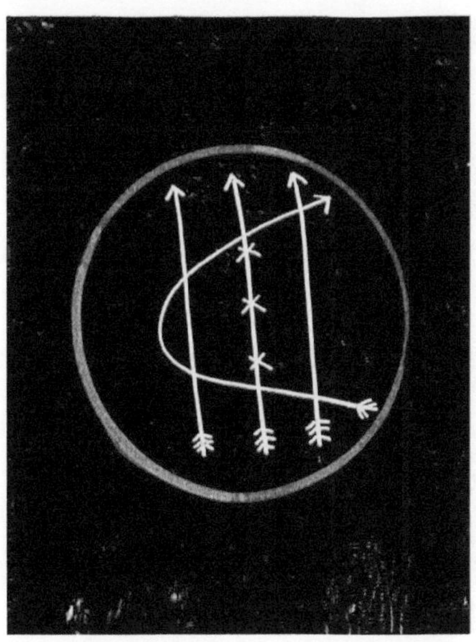

This particular spirit signature of Ozain is used in spells and rituals to open up the roads of success and opportunity for an individual.

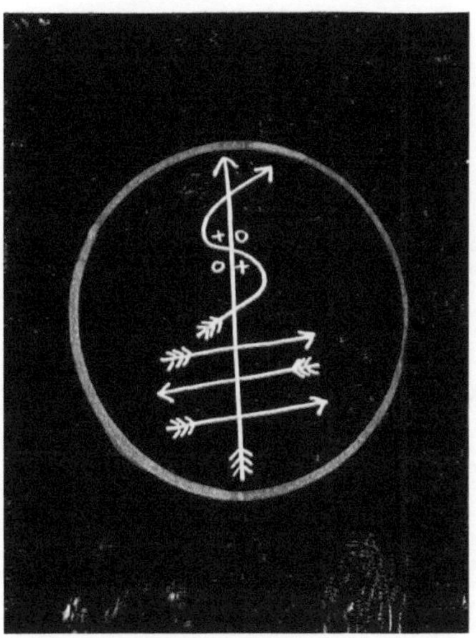

This particular spirit signature of Ozain is used in spells and rituals to change a bad situation into a positive situation.

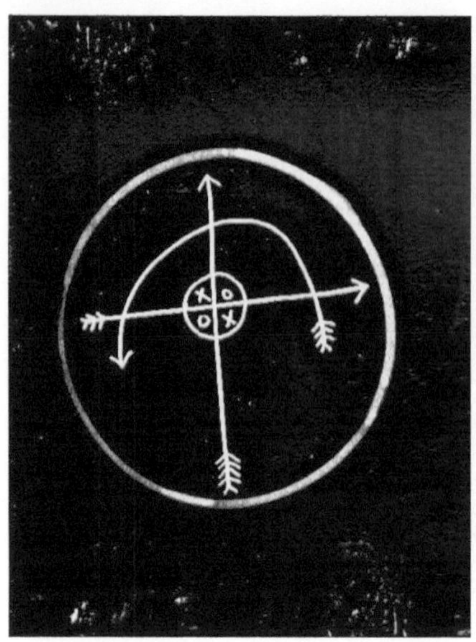

This particular spirit signature of Ozain is used in spells and rituals to attract love and romance.

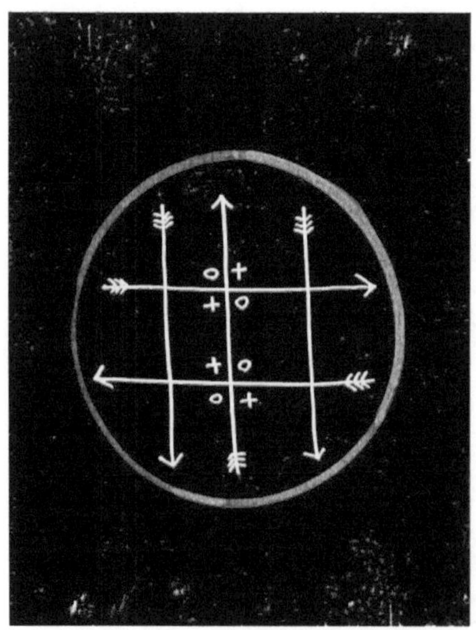

This particular spirit signature of Ozain is used in spells and rituals to make someone think about you or desire you.

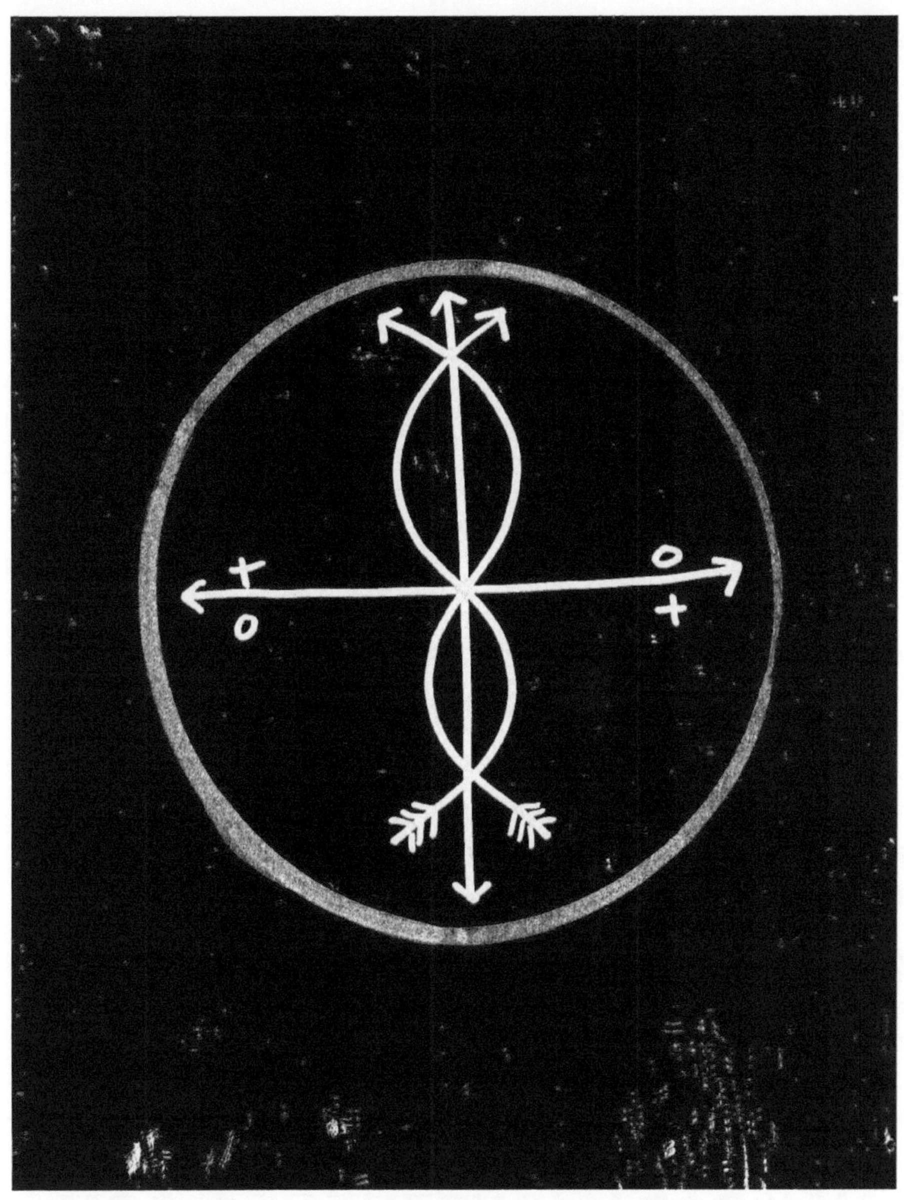

This particular spirit signature of Ozain is used in spells and rituals of protection or to make you invisible to your enemies.

SPIRITUAL OIL
SPIRITUAL OIL
SPIRITUAL OIL
SPIRITUAL OIL

www.ingramcontent.com/pod-product-compliance
Ingram Content Group UK Ltd.
Pitfield, Milton Keynes, MK11 3LW, UK
UKHW041925190726
13854UKWH00003B/1452